For
friend.

Roxy

Nobody Ever Offered Me Any Sausage!

Nobody Ever Offered Me Any Sausage!

THE WAY OF CONNECTING
WITH OURSELVES AND OTHERS

Roxy Harris DeCou, MSW BCD

OVER AND ABOVE
PRESS

Designed by Susan Shankin
Author photo by John Judge
Back cover photo by Damien Moody

Visit Roxy at www.roxydecou.com

To my three siblings Broni, Roy, and Cliff
who were my childhood playmates.

And to my three children Cyrelle, Vive, and Charles
who have made my adult life very interesting.

Acknowledgement

Jay S. Rosenblatt Ph.D., besides being an award winning scientist (the father of mothering), an excellent painter, psychoanalyst, professor of psychology at Rutgers University as well as Dean of Students, he was my 'Therp' (my very own therapist).

After three years, we terminated my treatment in the spring of 1971. That following fall when he returned from summer vacation, I was back in his office. This pattern was repeated for the next five years. I was unable to give him up until I moved to L.A. in 1976. As a parting gesture, I wrote this poem for him.

From 24 thru 32, the years of my life I have spent with you. When we first met, what can I say, I didn't know what was happening from day to day.

So, with little haste and excellent taste, you helped me put my life into place.

It took eight years of lots of pain, but if I had the chance I would do it again and again.

Now, here I am at 32 all grown up and no longer needing you.

Since then, Jay and I had stayed in touch as much as possible given that we lived on opposite coasts. Throughout the years, Jay encouraged me to write.

"Jay, it has taken me forty-five years to write this book." I wish I could share this moment with you.

(Jay S. Rosenblatt Ph.D. born November 18, 1924 and died on February 16, 2014 at age 90.)

Preface

This book is about combining the wisdom of the East and the West into a Zen-like self-help book.

My education and training were typically Western. I received a B.A. in psychology from Ohio State University, an M.S.W. from Hunter College, and trained at Albert Einstein College of Medicine in the Bronx. I earned a license to practice psychotherapy in California from the Board of Behavioral Sciences in 1981.

My life experience is not typically Western. In my early twenties, I was involved in Bioenergenic Therapy, a combination of working with the body and mind to help resolve emotional problems. This experience was the beginning of my realization that there was much more to learn about helping people than in traditional talk therapy. Practicing yoga, as well, added to my new awareness of the necessity of having a positive connection with our bodies.

Despite all my knowledge, I was unprepared in 1985 when I learned that my 42-year old sister was diagnosed with terminal cancer. I couldn't accept the reality of her dying and I became extremely depressed. I did the only thing I knew, I saw a psychiatrist. I asked him how to accept my sister's dying; his advice was "Don't think about it." Consequently, I sought treatment from five other mental health professionals, also to no avail.

Surprisingly, help came from Mary, my husband's bookkeeper. She was a devotee of a local guru, Prem Rawat, Maharaji, and invited me to go to a meeting. I was very skeptical, but since I was desperate and trusted her I went. Unaware at the time, going to that meeting was the beginning of my healing process.

Those wise people gave me the support I needed to accept reality instead of fighting it. They were available to me emotionally and over time with their help I was able to accept my sister's death.

Combining the "reason" of the West and the "intuition" of the East, I have conceptualized my own healing process. People come to me for help without knowing what is really troubling them. They complain about problems on the job and problems with their relationships. I encourage them to change their focus from the outside and to explore what is on the inside.

Once placing our focus on the inside, we begin to feel our pain and realize that our pain is rooted in our childhoods. Getting through childhood was an ordeal and we survived it any way we could. The more dysfunctional our parents were, the more pain we felt, and the more we carried shame for their abusive and neglectful behavior. We blamed ourselves for their inability to love us and we carry that shame throughout our lives.

In our sessions, my patients learn to shed this carried shame that was never theirs. Once this occurs they get in touch with their unmet needs for emotional intimacy. With my help, they learn how to get these needs met, and then they are able to find meaning and purpose in their lives.

Why I titled my book
"Nobody Ever Offered Me Any Sausage!"

Several months ago I asked my daughter's friend if he wanted breakfast. He said that he had already eaten sausage. When I replied, "Nobody ever offered me any sausage!" I was reminded that I always had to fend for myself. At that moment, it became the title for my book.

As a young child I believed in and trusted my mother and father without question. Their unrealities became my reality. What I believed growing up couldn't have been true because my parents' unrealities conflicted with each other. I realized that I only had myself to rely on. Along with the realization that I was on my own was a feeling of desperation. I was afraid that I would never be connected to anyone.

Now, I know that connecting with myself (becoming autonomous) is a necessity before I can connect with others. This connection to myself and others gives my life meaning.

I was born a first cousin of the chimps and bonobos. Unlike their natural environment, I was born into a set of expectations of others who would never know me. By the time I was 5 or 6, I had been put through a meat grinder and I became parts of parts of parts of myself, and no longer a part of nature.

For the next 6 or 7 years I attempted to survive by trying to please others. When I reached the age of 11 or 12, I began to realize how unhappy I was. I felt lost and alone. I did not feel that I belonged in my family or with people my own age. Though unaware, I tried to deny my pain by continuing to please or attempted to escape through drugs, sex, and alcohol. Some of us even try to please one moment, and the next behave recklessly. All in an attempt not to feel our pain. Many of us turn our rage against ourselves, and become anxious and depressed. We suffer in this unreality from feelings of helplessness and hopelessness, and may even become suicidal.

I know that reality is not the unreality that most people live in. Reality is what is. It is objective, we are subjective. The only way to know reality is by becoming an observer of our thoughts and feelings, and not a reactor to them.

We have a deep need for greater meaning in our lives and I have developed a way to connect to ourselves as well as to others. I share my insights with you through a process called Meditative Awareness Therapy. Through guided meditation with psychotherapy, my patients learn that they are not only their thoughts and feelings, which come and go, but a life force that is constant.

Once aware of this, we are present, and begin the process of finding a connection to ourselves and others. These connections are as necessary as sunlight and are the keys to living a healthy meaningful life.

Over the past several years, a collaboration between me and my patients has been occurring. I bring to our sessions my life's work and experience, and they bring their budding awareness, together the following insights have come to life.

I now serve you a platter of Roxygrams, some are easily digested, other's need to be chewed well, and some will be hard to swallow. They all need to be savored over time.

We are starved for reality and
awareness satiates our hunger.

2

Find my pain.

Find my soul.

Find my passion.

3

A relationship is two fucked up people

trying not to kill each other.

I live to surrender,

and hope to die with dignity.

5

If I watch my behavior,

I will know who I am.

6

Only when I am not attending to
my thoughts or feelings, am I aware.

7

I belong

wherever I am.

8

How I feel is never an excuse

for how I behave.

9

Being happy and having fun

are not the reasons to be.

10

As children become adults,

adults become children.

11

Only when I get out of my way,

am I able to see who else is in it.

12

The more dysfunctional
our childhoods were,
the greater need
we have to be perfect.

13

As long as I want my mother to grow up,
I will stay a child.

As long as I wait for my mother to love me,
I will stay a child.

14

I can love and hate

the same person.

15

Children are victims

by definition.

16

Complaining is a way

of getting attention.

17

My future depends upon

my living well now.

18

I must give up my carried shame

in order to embrace my child within.

19

I live to express

not to impress.

20

Being good enough

is way good enough.

21

My feelings give me information.

The information is to

be judged not the feelings.

22

Until I get in touch with my rage,
I will be controlled by my fear of it.

23

Being loved as a child is crucial
to becoming a loving adult.

24

If I accept what is,

I am present.

25

There are no good or bad children,

only good or bad parents.

26

I love you because you are like me,
I hate you because you are like me.

I love you because you are not like me,
I hate you because you are not like me.

27

An infant knows that
abandonment means death.
An adult knows that abandonment
only feels like death.

28

People believe that they are rational,
without any awareness that their unconscious
controls their lives.

29

I create drama instead
of feeling my pain.

30

I will never feel good enough
until I lower my expectations.

Before I can lower my expectations,
I must know what they are.

31

Truth is revealed in

our connection to nature.

32

I am a victim of my unstructured life.

I am a victim of my overly structured life.

33

When I ask a question,
I need attention or the answer.

34

How I feel is not to be judged,

how I behave is.

35

If I can't hate,

I can't love.

36

As a child I did not feel loved and
blamed myself for not being worthy.

37

The more I care about myself,

the better care I take of myself.

38

The only thing to aspire to

is self-acceptance.

39

Everything I know

is from my experience,

and from my experience

I know reality.

40

It's great to be aware
that I am not a victim.
Now I have total
responsibility for my life.

41

I must be aware of my intentions

for every word I utter

and every move I make.

42

All relationships end,

there are no failures.

43

Being a victim and feeling like one
aren't necessarily the same.

44

It's not the feedback I get from others,

it's what I feed myself that matters.

45

Freedom is the
absence of worry.

46

I was drowning in shame,

now I am swimming with confidence.

47

In order to have a meaningful life,

I must stop making excuses

for not having one.

48

When we are healthy emotionally,

we are authentic.

Otherwise, we act as if.

49

It's not only what happens to me,
it's how I deal with what happens to me.

50

How much I live in my head is directly related to how much shame I feel.

51

I keep wandering around my central self.

I keep wondering around my central self.

52

Parents are obligated to their children,
not the other way around.

53

I am indulging in one addiction
or another instead of embracing my pain.

54

To be authenic,

I need to feel my pain.

55

Falling in love calls up all
my unmet needs of childhood.

56

I cannot get my basic intimacy
needs met if I am too vulnerable or
not vulnerable enough.

57

I must get my satisfaction

from the efforts I make, since I may not

have control over the results.

58

My thoughts come and go.

My feelings come and go.

I must depend upon the

present moment for comfort.

59

In order to have a meaningful
relationship with anyone,
I must have one with myself first.

60

Since I have become an adult

I am the only one who can validate me.

61

I can't trust my thoughts or feelings

to make decisions,

my judgement is what I must rely on.

62

When I feel rage and terror
at the same time,
I may have a panic attack.

63

Only when I embrace

my deepest painful feelings,

may I be free from my carried shame.

64

We must do what is right
no matter how hard it is.

65

It may take forever
before behaving
courageously feels good.

66

I am nobody's audience

and nobody is mine.

67

When my thoughts and feelings

fight for supremacy,

I loose.

68

I can trust my experiences

not my thoughts.

69

Our need for connections

is as vital as our needs

for air, water, and food.

70

Don't expect to be comfortable
until you are dead.

71

My fear of abandonment

makes me a phony.

72

As I become more self-aware,

I get closer to nature.

73

How I feel is never an excuse

for how I behave.

74

As a child, I was a victim.

As an adult, I victimize myself.

75

Life is about finding
balance in everything.

76

Feeling helpless and enraged is
an immobilizing combination resulting
in depression or violence.

77

The world is not going to captain my ship,

and if it does I better watch out.

78

Children bring out the best
and the worst in their parents.

79

To be aware is to be present.

To be present is to be aware.

80

Unless I am connected to nature,

I'm not grounded.

81

My awareness transforms me
without being aware
of the transformation.

82

Through my growing awareness
the possibility exists that I may
transform into a person I admire.

83

I am good enough

whether or not

I feel good enough.

84

Once I have a connection to myself,

I won't live in terror of

being abandoned by another.

85

Body language tells the truth.

Words lie.

86

Self-acceptance is the
bedrock of our lives.

87

My needs do not get met by
meeting someone else's needs.

88

Our thoughts rationalize

our feelings away.

89

I am righteous
about my addictions,
and self-righteous
about other's addictions.

90

If we don't take risks,

we can't live fully.

91

We are all basically the same
except for the manner in which
we survived childhood.

92

What adults tolerate
is what they deserve.

93

The manner in which we
are victimized as children may
predict how as adults
we victimize ourselves and others.

94

Get the fuck out of your head
and into your body!

95

I was taught that if I loved my mother

I would go to heaven, and

if I hated her I would go to hell.

96

Without a stable foundation
of self-acceptance,
I am lost.

97

As long as I carry shame,

I cannot know reality.

98

The more self-respect I have,

the more respectful I will be of others.

99

Being present is safe,

being in my head is dangerous.

100

Surviving childhood makes
it almost impossible
to live fully as an adult.

101

My weaknesses I must embrace,

other's weaknesses

I must steer clear of.

102

We must be vigilant about living in reality, given our crazy-making childhoods.

103

How I feel at any one moment

is not as important

as how I feel about myself.

104

When I am dead I will be perfect,
until then I will be human.

105

I never got enough,

now I cannot get enough.

I got more than enough,

now I cannot get enough.

106

The connection to ourselves and others
is what gives our lives meaning.

107

Living in your head makes
you feel safe and drives you crazy
at the same time.

108

If I live in reality,

I may be able to affect it.

If I don't live in reality,

I'm at the mercy of it.

109

No matter how I feel,

I am still good enough.

110

Who said thoughts
are more rational
than feelings?

111

To be fully alive

we must shed our shame,

both carried and self-imposed.

112

The only real difference
among us is how we defend
ourselves against our pain.

113

Adults who can say NO

do not get used or abused.

114

I must embrace my feelings
instead of reacting to them.

115

Time to give up,

not to give in.

116

I can read 100 books

on how to swim,

but

never get the courage

to jump in the water.

117

I am a victim of my own
thoughts and feelings.

118

No matter how old I am,

I can only take baby steps.

119

My feelings control my life

whether or not

I am in touch with them.

120

My thoughts do little else
other than tell me
that I am not good enough.

121

If I need to be better
than good enough,
I lack self-acceptance.

122

I must validate myself
from the inside out,
not the outside in.

123

I am a slave to my need to be needed.

I am also the master of that slave.

124

Accepting my pain

is accepting myself.

125

Once I have accepted my pain,

I have a connection

to myself and others.

126

Living is not an
intellectual experience.

127

If I can't say no,

I can't say yes.

128

What was was, what is is,
and the rest is unknowable.

129

One day is little different from another,

other than the drama I create.

130

Complaining is creating drama.

131

Relationships die if
conflicts are not resolved.

132

The more abusive my childhood,

the more shame I feel,

the more self-destructive I may become.

133

As adults, we try to get
our needs met as if
we were still children.

134

If I am half a cake,

I need the other half.

If I am a whole cake,

I only need icing.

135

Our need to be perfect

is directly related to how

much shame we carry.

136

Our dreams are here and now.

Our thoughts and feelings

come from the past.

137

CHILDHOOD

I live in fear.

I live in fear of others.

I live in fear of other's rage.

TRANSITION

I live in fear.

I live in fear of myself.

I live in fear of my rage.

ADULTHOOD

I am free from fearing other's rage.

I am free from fearing my rage.

I AM FREE!

A wise New York Jew once said,
"If something is true 96% of the time,
it is true enough."

Roxygrams are like physical and mathematical constants. They give us insight into reality and withstand the scrutiny of all honest inquiry. Thus, they are true regardless of what any of us may think.

That is not to say that they are evident. It takes discipline and fortitude to recognize the diamond of a fundamental truth within the rough of a simple statement. As sentient beings we hunger for truths and this book is the guide for all to see that they are not alone.

—Pete Chudykowski,
Software Engineer

47096099R00163

Made in the USA
Charleston, SC
28 September 2015